Slamming & Splitting

Poems

Catherine Arra

CONTENTS

She Says

A crazy woman
       lives in the attic.

She scribbles on walls
scratches at the door.
       At night
       her room glows, though no light or candle burns.

She says
       it's the fire in her bowels she can't put out.

We worry
       the neighbors will notice, and then
the house is so hot and balmy
smelling of her, we must open the windows.

When I go out I wear big hats.

She likes
       the blue velvet one best.
       It's soft she says.

She wants
       my hair loose and wild, like a
       lion's mane, and summer when clothing is skimpy
       so her skin can breathe.

She says she needs to breathe
       and complains about the compact car, the stuffy bedroom
       ceilings and the new housekeeper.

She says
       she's sure he's having an affair with her.

Last week she tore down
       all the wallpaper and moved to the attic.

Now she's terrified of cellophane.
       She resists bathing

and condoms - that slimy, taut latex chokes her.

"Someday
      I'll bust through," she says,
       "and burn this damned house down."

Traffic

At the Second Avenue Deli, the hot pastrami on rye tasted good
really good, though it blew her diet, was too much salt
and she was interrupted

by having to put another quarter in the meter. She found
her car blocked, stuck between a double parked flatbed
and a rusted Buick. She wondered

if owning a car in New York, the drive downtown
the two pounds on tomorrow's scale
and the chance she might not make it back
for her 2:00 were worth it.

But she hated mass transportation. It made her feel dirty
and submissive. He adored the city

was the reason she lived in it, was why traffic had
become her daily challenge. She could never wash

his air off her face. It stuck to her like grease
on an exhaust fan. No combination
of soaps or creams worked.

At night she imagined the urban hum
as surf, the flicker of streetlights as fireflies

that he was someone who once
wanted the taste of her
on his tongue like good pastrami.

She deposited a quarter in the meter, turned the lever
and calculated that the two or three foot space between her car
and the next might be sufficient for a carefully negotiated out.

She finished her sandwich and the German ale but found the car
was still a problem. She cursed the flatbed

bumped the Buick and executed
nearly fourteen three-point turns, grinding first gear to reverse and a

marginal escape.

That night she told him she was leaving and left
checked into a nearby hotel.

The next morning she walked
to work, stopped to buy a coffee to go.
Outside she licked the visible air

and thought it tasted good, really good.

Ghost

She said I abandoned you
and fed your loss.
Do you know, now?
Is that why you
wake me from slumber, shattering sleep
a fire ax against the glass of forgetting?

Do you wish to tell me
but can't speak? Can't act? A dislodged dream figure
trapped in these predawn hours after the snow storm
circling in woods, white and moonless.
Mute until there appears the shadowy apparition
of a house, its corners and long sloping roof.
The outline of the three-windowed room
where you wrote your opus, stoic and solitary
in other winters long ago or this one?

Could that be you, the man in the window
legs extended, keyboard lapped
staring into a naked landscape, blind and bound to task?
He doesn't notice the woman sitting in the kitchen below
two candles flickering on the page
on her face
where words form and fade
until she catches them, writes them down.

She's lonely.
He doesn't see, but you do.
You must go to her and tell her.
Find the path to the door. It's here
under snowfall. You feel the firmness of the stones.
Yes here, and you must find the door
open it quickly, climb the stairs and insist
he stop now. Put the work aside
get up from the chair, pull himself from the glow
of the computer and tell her
he knows, now.

But you are frozen in

an icy sculpture. You howl to him, to her
but sound is snowed under with grass
and dirt, with her sleeping flowers
planted just outside his window for beauty
for color while he worked.

You whimper inside crystal armor
terrified by the landscape that has made you.
You twist, turn, pound. Holler and hurl
against memory's vault until you wake
in a January sweat, in a city far away
scalded in streetlight, clamoring with traffic
and she says
"Shh, shh now. It's nothing.
A bad dream is all."
Just as the woman in the kitchen
lays down her pen.

The Collapsed Woman

No longer sees herself
follows the dots of each day
dressed in trend, shimmered
in lipstick, one good coat of mascara.
Picture perfect, pretty as the cliché, prettier
because she's competitive too.

She is ever and always so sure of herself
a real "know-it-all," coy
with a feminine blush, her argument seductive.

She's good, really good at her game.
So good, she doesn't know the game has her.
She's an easy target, easy prey
easy and easily fooled.
Predators circle; she's an exquisite host for parasites.

Collapsed, she is a distortion of herself
and believes it, feeds it, suckles it.
Until one night during the final dissent into winter
a series of shocks, lightning bolts emanating
from the heart in her brain, begin
and double exponentially in number and charge
until they mix with tears and trembling
compound into thunderstorms, hurricanes, tsunamis
and electrocute her, hurtling her out of death
into a stitched up, patched up reincarnation
like an unsuspecting Frankenstein.

All alone, not another of her kind to be found.

Things That Collapse

Sunflowers in mid-September
heavy heads bowed low to the roots
of crippled stems.

A seventy-foot maple
under the chainsaw's wedge.

The temples of antiquity
when pagan gods fell to the order of one.

A cardboard box
flattened corner by corner.

Fruits and vegetables
too long without water.

Balloons, lungs, old skin.

An ocean wave rolled to a hiss.
An avalanche waterfalled, dominos downed
sand sculptures.

The horses in *Gone With the Wind* and *True Grit*.

A universe that stops expanding
a body that stops breathing.
A marriage.

Married but Separated : Apology

They sit at a green table
with a vase of white Alstroemeria
a white votive candle
goat cheese, olive tapenade, crackers.
She opens the Pinot Noir he brought
fills crystal glasses.
From dusky twilight outside the window
they are a still life.

He talks about his day, his haircut, did she notice?
He tells her how hard it is now, staying organized
remembering everything he needs to do.
The mundane defeats him.

She smiles, admires the haircut
sympathizes with the squeeze of the job she remembers well.
He forgets she did it too, for longer and with more.

She places salmon on an alder wood plank
sets it in the oven to roast, starts the risotto.
A woodsy aroma fills the kitchen. She offers
a new poem. He listens.
Then like a slingshot he breathes in
exhales with finger pointed and roars
"How do you expect me to react to a line like that?"

The sharp yellow glint in his eyes stuns her.
They are frozen in their familiar severance
polarized with guns drawn.

She says
"This is not about you."
gathers the pages, stands.
"Don't tell me what to write."

She leaves the table, flowers, candle, the wine.
He sits in the space she makes.

She stirs the risotto.

She plates the food
positions his steaming dish before him
fills the glasses.
She tastes her effort. It's good.
But he's not eating.
In all their years he'd dive headlong into the food
left hand clenched around the stem of the wine glass
fork like a backhoe in the other hand.
Sometimes he'd say it was good.
Most times, so accustomed to
that steaming plate of predictability
he hardly noticed one meal from another.

It filled him up, served him. Made life easier.

Tonight he sits in silence, looking at the pale green plate
        with roasted salmon
        creamy risotto
        grilled asparagus
        as if a mirror.
He studies it, lets fragrant heat rise to meet him
before he lifts the first forkful to lips.

She watches his regret like reversed digestion
rise up with steam
from bowels, to throat
to tongue and meet his first taste
of understanding loss.

Then he savors every slow mouthful.

Married but Separated: Prayer

We hammered those long, green
phallic-looking spikes into the warm, moist sod
to feed the mountain laurels, the magnolia
the white Rose of Sharon planted
for my mother, sprinkled with a handful of her ashes
and circled with sea stones smuggled
from the shoreline where we let
the rest of her go.

     Do you remember how she stayed with us
     swirled around our toes in that shimmering inlet
     tucked between boulders and wild sea roses?
     How she lingered and waited among
     the great sculpted rock of the New Hampshire coast?
     How she seemed to kiss us
     thankful for her deliverance?
     How other worldly it was, watching
     her dusty body reform
     and leave with the swell of tide.

In the backyard grotto, you knelt
to fertilize the Kenyan dogwood
we planted for our marriage, there
under its nascent boughs
eleven years ago now.
I knelt beside you pretending
to mark the spot for the green spike
but prayed
swirling in the ashes of our history
imagining a thousand white blooms next June
a broad canopy of flora and leaf
and roots that don't let go.

     When we turned to leave the sea's edge
     the wind had blown a spray of her ashes back to you.
     They marked the center of your forehead
     like the burnt palms that mark the season of Lent.
     Is this too a mother's blessing
     and these, our days of sacrifice before rebirth?

Married but Separated: This Year, This Time

Last year, this time they did not speak.
She flew to Florida, he drove to Carolina
their lives together undone in explosions
and crossfire cultivated
over the trajectory of years.
It was a terrific crescendo and crash.
Clothes hurled to the driveway
in aerobic fits of temper and trembling.
Out, out, this failure of love
this naked, flayed, raw vulnerability
sliced skin thin
laid out in embarrassing display.
It was Christmas, last Christmas
and it became their lacuna like a vortex in space
a wormhole furrowed over years through which
they must go.

While and then came
lawyers, summons, complaints, actions
fees, property, taxes, agreements
all served in an indigestible buffet.
The legalese of lost love is tragic.
Yet, she couldn't stop herself
from buying him jeans or loving him in her rage.
He went monastic, or pretended to
surrendered everything
for grace and a used Cadillac.
The lawyer claimed he was unstable
"to strike while the iron's hot," but maybe
this was his chosen penance, his prayer
a quest to make them whole, at last.
Believing more in the likelihood of human greed
than grace, she signed the papers
and collapsed to her knees.
The woman lost in the mirror of another self
stared hard from the silver, demanding
recognition.

This year, this time

she flew to Florida, he followed.
Traversing miles of exile
she entered again the snow globe of their former life
kissed him in swirling glitter.
She believed
and never believed
he would slam her again
six months later, this year, this time
with the same lie.

Without a Crumb

What does it mean, riddled?
He is riddled with doubt, the poor soul is
riddled with cancer, riddled with bullets
like Bonnie & Clyde, peppered down dead.
She is riddled with laughter, tickled with riddles.
Speak in riddles, riddle me a riddle:
Will the stumped tree ever sprout again?
Write me a riddle, I'll give you a rhyme
school-yard time like hide and seek
kick the can under the swing. Don't peek.
Give me a riddle, I'll pay you a dime
rhymes with you show me yours
I'll show you mine.

Take this tangle too, this knotted old chain
riddled around an abandoned gold ring.
Lay down the compass, the calculated design
love is not a riddle, doesn't need to rhyme.
Find us a path in this sylvan spring
raspberry maples sexing lashes to the robin sky
lime-gold filigree haloing bark
laugh with me, run with me, make a new start.
Un-riddle the diddle: why don't we work?
Can you, will you
give us a nearing in the clearing to love
riddled with love like dandelion art?
Go on now, raise your thumb
the sky is darkening and we haven't a crumb.
See the dead rabbit riddled with bugs?
The black crow caws and the hawk circles.

Riddle me a riddle, husband mine,
and I'll sing you this rhyme.

Rag

It was a mistake to mend his favorite shirt
giving him license to make her want
to tear it again.

She should have left it
uncollared and buttonless
to remind him twice is beyond repair.

When He Is Again Unkind

I plant herbs: a trio of mint, oregano, basil
Provence lavender for the purple smell and parsley.
I haul to the patio the ten-pound rosemary that wintered
in my classroom the last six years on the job, this winter
in the study upstairs. I saw off three inches from the dense root ball
add new soil to new space.

I feed and groom my dead mother's cat, now
my brother's cat, but away on vacation, I go twice each day.
She recognizes mother's intonations, looks up
with surprised ears. I speak to her in expressions Mom used.
It's sad and comforting for me and the cat.

I make an arugula salad, grill filets and asparagus
for my best friend and me. We drink good wine, talk about art:
when to paint things, say things
leave space and wait.

Before my husband and I separated
into this year-long, teetering on the knife-edge of divorce, I used
to sneak ingredients into the 20-minute recipe of every argument
always a pinch too sweet, a dash too salty, a drop more or less acrid.

I cannot retrieve the irretrievable
I cannot bring back the dead
but I can feed the rosemary, give it space
I can select spices, dine quietly. And before
I go to sleep, I can paint my toenails sweetheart pink.

Mistaken Symmetry

At night she dreams. Is she dreaming?
She slides through sifting sand, under an undertow
to the other?

Her heart slows
with each mammoth shift of Earth.
She exhumes air in tunneled rasps
like a woman nearly drowned - an inverted roar until each cell fills.

It happened again this afternoon on the chaise lounge, in mid-sun
a glimpse.
Last week during the pedicure, lulled to a vibrating threshold
strong, small hands massaging her soles
she slipped through

looked from eyes closed, past the pink membrane
as a fetus might from blood-soaked tissue.

Who is she in that other universe?
Would she recognize herself, be her best friend?
What life has she lived there
and with whom?

She strains to hear the coral conversation
imagines an isotropic reach.

Sub Space Fractures

The universe tilts.

The carefully drawn line

      on the *Etch a Sketch*
      breaks
            and
            disintegrates.

All that was focused blurs
      or all that was blurred
is suddenly crisp with hallucinogenic clarity.

It happened the day
      his father died on the golf course, the
      minute the car hit the dog
      the afternoon she left him, and

he's wandered around the supermarket ever since, hoping
he'd bump into her between the band aids and strawberries.

It happened the day
      the earth split and split again
      killing 5,000 along with her son, the morning the blood test
      came back positive.

It happened the spring
      she fell in love
      the February she pawned his ring.

But what of the spaces between points of memory
      and the tattoos formed therein?

Like this lives are inked with skulls and crossbones,
      hearts and lightning bolts.

Like this we bleed through the fractures
      and so are marked.

Slamming & Splitting

In 1913, Niels Bohr made a metaphor
       reached across decades to a fifth-grade girl.

His atom with its nucleus of protons and neutrons
       chalked on the blackboard in blue and pink
       danced inside dances of yellow electrons.

Frenetic particles and their dizzy arcs
       dangled before her like ornaments.

It's pretty, she thought.
       She would remember it
not the science - the idea, the unwritten law
making it appear so and somehow obeyed.

       Even Einstein agreed and
       called Bohr's atom music.

Living, she discovered, was a theory
       of something like atoms
       a super-collider adventure of slamming and splitting
       speeding and slowing, of annihilating parts
       back to primordial silence.

No matter
       Bohr's picture was blasted out of contention
       twelve years after he drew it.

No matter
       it was replaced with no picture at all - a condition
       like poetry before it's written.

Stuff in the Bottom

An email address for Peter K:
    did my web page last year.
The bottom part of a clothes hanger
    you know, the kind that's not supposed to crease your pants
    but only the bottom. One sock.
A photo from Middletown
    where I taught 5, no 6 years ago
of the Latin Club, run by Nilda, a friend then.

A Spanish fan, a woman's
    Umm, my mother's, I think.
The town of Gardiner schedule and transfer station fees.
    A pair of foot pads, Dr. Scholl's.
A Basotho flag, one a kid drew for me;
    he knew I lived there.
    South Africa. It's in South Africa
A championship pennant, one we won for 2nd or 3rd place
    with the REUR - Recreational Euro Youth Activities.

A Japanese structure, well, a laminated picture
    of a Japanese structure built in water.
Stars: silver, red, blue, green, gold.
Your poem, *Leaving Sicilia* in English and Italian, a little crumpled
    but I'd better not tell you that.

Some ancient knitting instrument,
    a handle with a hook on the end.
Going to sort these things out; some need a place.

A Jiffy phrase book, Italian, key survival phrases
    yes, like *attenta* and *auito.*
A wood screw, another wood screw.

The week in Germany
    a tie rack, a penny.

Tomorrow I'm leaving here to live at the bottom of a mountain
    next to a swamp.

I have a broom and no dustpan.

And someday I'll have this poem you made for me
found in the bottom of the closet
among the things of my next passage
        and perhaps I'll take it with me.

The Lone Hollow Who

Birdsong recital
> pre-dawn cacophony
> a dozen, no two dozen chirping pianos, or
> one baby grand keyed by a dozen hands.
> Crickets keening in the pedals.

Day laborer next door
> slams the door, starts the truck
> a dog barks
> NPR radio alarms, 5:15 a.m.

I lay in white down, between white sheets
> review today's list, Wednesday.
> Rehearse, I will

Will my life to live
> outside the confessional, the dark polished pine
> penance prayed and granted
> the screen door closed.

Disrobed, your secrets gut me
> like the plaintive call
> of the mourning dove
> hollowing sweet noise
> to a dead silence.

Night Passage

I wake each night
as if by death knell
to rise in sleep and attend
this funeral.

Weeks now, months, years?
How long have I slept in the skin
of mourning, unable to look in mirrors
listened to the eulogy as it's written, each night
counted flowers on a casket in a boat
crossing water?

On the shoreline, a silhouette
caped in a wilderness of loss
grieves and watches, swallows infinity.

Or is it I who cross
and you the cloaked figure
on the other shore?

To be Delivered to the Assigned Justice
for Issue of Divorce by June 27

Lone bird
in green leaves
dense
summer
after rain
fan
up
sifting air
down
to still-
ness.

Call
in the wood
what song,
what caller?
Lone bird
what
what
what?

Fly
zips
figure 8
side vision-
zing.

Milkweed surf-
glides
geraniums
curl
away
mid sun
spinning spider
waits.

Black ant
staggers

dead bee
bluestone
step.

17-year
cicadas
maracas jam
shelled
hushed.

Lone bird
sings
leaves.

Screen Saver

Sparks and fiery piñatas, serpents
and drunken spider webs. An electric crab

cuts across my dozing screen. I'm certain there
is a pattern, a sequence that repeats itself, but the
program is long, has countless variations
is too subtle in its transitions.

I've studied it for hours, taken copious notes. I've
measured the shifts in configurations, timed the length
of cycles, mapped the location of each new star burst.

I keep a journal, have a Master's degree, attend
night classes for my Ph.D. I read Jung and Freud
Physics Today. I believe in God and the Tarot
meditate, hesitate, fall in and out of love.

Every year I grow older and tally my days
determined to break the code, analyze the plan
but I can't decipher the Ion storm
anymore than the trajectory of depression, the

virus of passion or the ache of trying
to save myself.

Syndrome

Trying to stay married
        trying to stay
        at all

was the constant drone
        of rain
        drowning potted herbs

        downing dogwood petals.

Noise
gunfire on glass

drumsticks hammering the snare

the single drop of torture
        to the temple.

Thing Is

Here's the thing:
  a microscopic organism, call it
  a parasite - this invisible creature
  birthed from another invisible creature.

Call it
  need, hunger, want, fear
  the smallest sub-atomic particle, dark matter

  a mother's touch,
  father's approval
  equal notice, fair share, any share
  a morsel, a drop
  air.

Anything please, anything
but an empty plate.

Consumes itself, must
eat its non-essential organs
then its very essence
  survives and dies, and lives
  the living dead, gothic, hidden, sightless

eyeless ground mole grubbing to light
squirming down under panicked discovery
  the porn freak, alcoholic, stoner, thief
  gambler, binger, liar, cheat.

Name it, it's there
  at the addict's table
  eating its way

to a girlfriend, boyfriend
  husband, wife
a sub-space familiar required to
pay alms, give penance, sustain again
the original wound
  absolve the sin.

They say it's a psychological thing.

Sucking begins as seduction - Mmm
  caress, soothe, suck, slap, caress
  suck, Mmm, suck, Mmm, suck
  slap, caress
  slap, slap, slap
A morphine drip
  syncopated, reversed.

The host offers itself, did you know? Yes
  to serve its predator at all cost
  a dear price, especially
  in marriage - the vow practically
  says so.

No, easier to lose a pint or two of blood
know when to cut your losses, fold with a full house
sacrifice the bet.

Divorce Pearls

Letting go still loving, still

      is like passing a kidney stone

the calcified biology of loving
spun hard over churning years
grinding through a single portal

      the worst kind of internal bleeding
      no matter how microscopic.

I want to gather the stones
      of loving, leaving & letting go

string them all together
      this is one.

        * * *

Avanti in Italian means, come in,
      come ahead, go forward, in front.
Exact translation, impossible.

At Avanté, a hair salon, a spin on the Italian
      scalp slathered with dye

the phone sings, displays: lawyer's office
      to say divorce signed Tuesday.

(I count 1, 2, 3 days ago...what was I doing, Tuesday...
      did I feel something, did I know?)

Remind myself, I set this in motion
      the tick, tock, the sick, numb
a choice in answer to all of his choices.

Are the scales balanced?
justice served?

Something about the sterile sword
        the last cut.

Exact translation, impossible.

                    * * *

I want a new life, a new name
        a cat's nine lives.

How to shed, molt
        textbook the history
        box & delete.

How to forget
        when layers bubble up
        like lava from a forgotten core

and swallow hard.

                    * * *

There had to be an end, a death
        ceremony, burial

a cremation & casting of bones
        like fairy dust bouquets

ghosts swirling in a miscalculated relativity.

                    * * *

Another night of the usual:
        sleep for 2
wake,   sleep
        wake, shivered, alone
        each time
swaddled in a sweating sorrow.

                    * * *

And then it happened
        free falling, flat-backed, boom down
        a fainting death.

Twice
the aperture pin-holed to black
twice, I spiraled through the only universe I know
        & then the one I don't.

Three hard blows to the head
        tooth cut below the lip.

When I can see again
        I see my father cupping air above me
        trembling.
Please , please he says, *wake her up*

        Wake her up.

           * * *

        There is
        a crescent-moon scar
        under my lip
        like a pink tattoo.

           * * *

Yoga teacher says:

Set an intention
give your practice today to another... give the light, the love.

Breathe it in... breathe it out
three OMs to seal your intention.

        I danced
        for you
        on
        &
        off

the red mat

gave you all
with
grace
&
gratitude

Breathe in, **Let***...breathe out,* **Go**

respira…respira…respira…

About the Author

Catherine Arra is a native of the Hudson Valley in upstate New York where she taught public school English and writing for 34 years. In 2012, she retired and now divides her time between New York and the Space Coast of Florida. *Slamming & Splitting,* her first chapbook, was a winner in the Red Ochre Press chapbook contest and was published in 2014. This second edition is available through Amazon, CreateSpace, and Barnes and Noble. Her second chapbook, *Loving from the Backbone*, a collection of love poems, (Flutter Press, 2015) is available through Amazon and CreateSpace. Arra's poetry and prose can be found in *The Timberline Review, Boston Literary Magazine, Rose Red Review, Wildness,* and *Pioneertown* among other journals and anthologies online and in print.
Contact: Carra22@aol.com

www.ingramcontent.com/pod-product-compliance
Lightning Source LLC
Chambersburg PA
CBHW020445030426
42337CB00014B/1396